KFK KINGFISHER KNOWLEDGE

DINOSAURS

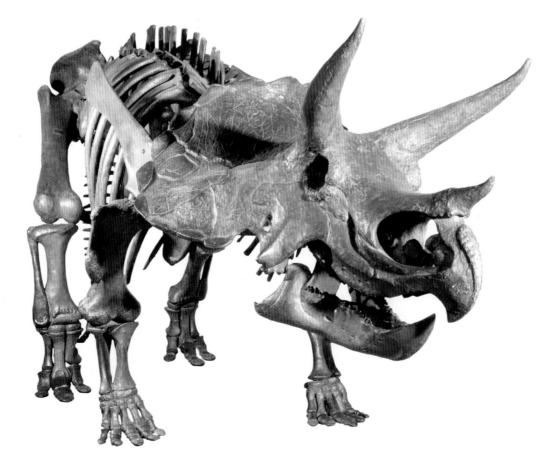

◀ This fossil skeleton belongs to a small, predatory dinosaur called *Coelophysis*. It lived in what is now the southwestern USA more than 220 million years ago.

KFK KINGFISHER KNOWLEDGE

DINOSAURS

Nigel Marven

KINGFISHER

Additional text: Dougal Dixon
Editor: Clare Hibbert
Designers: Peter Clayman, Rebecca Painter
Consultant: Dr Phil Manning, School of Earth, Atmospheric and
 Environmental Sciences, University of Manchester
Picture research manager: Cee Weston-Baker
Senior production controller: Lindsey Scott
DTP manager: Nicky Studdart
Proofreader and indexer: Polly Goodman

KINGFISHER

Kingfisher Publications Plc, New Penderel House,
283–288 High Holborn, London WC1V 7HZ
www.kingfisherpub.com

First published by Kingfisher Publications Plc 2007
10 9 8 7 6 5 4 3 2 1

1TR/0607/TWP/MA(MA)/130ENSOMA/F

ISBN: 978 07534 1474 3

GO FURTHER...
INFORMATION PANEL KEY:

websites and
further reading

career paths

places to visit

Contents

NOTE TO READERS
The website addresses listed in this book are correct at the time of going to print. However, due
to the ever-changing nature of the internet, website addresses and content can change. Websites
can contain links that are unsuitable for children. The publisher cannot be held responsible for
changes in website addresses or content, or for information obtained through third-party
websites. We strongly advise that internet searches should be supervised by an adult.

▼ Plesiosaurs were large marine reptiles that
swam in the world's waters from around 200
million years ago until 65 million years ago.

Foreword

Dinosaur – one of the most thrilling words in the English language! It conjures up images of a prehistoric past when the world was ruled by great reptiles. Some were ferocious predators; others, gentle giants. This book provides a glimpse of their world. I became interested in dinosaurs because of my passion for smaller reptiles. Ever since I can remember I've had a menagerie of cold-blooded pets, from geckos to giant tortoises. It's wonderful to think that some of today's reptiles were around in dinosaur times. And when I watch my lizards feeding, displaying to each other or laying eggs, they give clues to how dinosaurs behaved.

My job as a wildlife presenter gave me a chance to get even closer to dinosaurs. The makers of *Walking with Dinosaurs* asked if I could join them to travel back in time to meet computer-generated *Tyrannosaurus rex*, *Protoceratops*, *Argentinosaurus*, plesiosaurs and more. They needed a person to give scale to their creations, and many of the creatures I came to know so well are featured in this book. To get our facts right, we relied on teams of palaeontologists (dinosaur experts). I learnt so much about the Triassic, Jurassic and Cretaceous – the periods when Earth was dominated by dinosaurs.

Of course, without a time machine nobody can be sure how dinosaurs looked. As you'll see on page 40, dinosaur scales are occasionally preserved, but fossils never reveal the true colours of their skin, so we can't tell if dinosaurs were green, brown, orange, red or blue. But by seeing how modern animals camouflage themselves, or get dazzling colours in the breeding season, we can make reasonable guesses. Sounds don't fossilize either, so we don't know if *Tyrannosaurus rex* roared or if *Triceratops* bellowed, but fossils do give clues about calls, as you'll see on page 41.

Making the television films also gave me an insight into dinosaur habitats. The film-makers tried to choose landscapes with just the right vegetation. Grass would never do – it didn't evolve until long after dinosaurs became extinct. Monkey puzzle trees are perfect because their close relatives have been around for some 300 million years. To film the right background for my adventures with *Tyrannosaurus rex*, we went to Chile in South America, home to some of the last remaining monkey puzzle forests.

Fraser Island in Australia is another good substitute for prehistoric landscapes. It has vast sand dunes that look exactly like the Mongolian deserts inhabited by *Protoceratops* and *Velociraptor*. You can read about a famous fossil of these two dinosaurs fighting on page 21. Fraser Island also has forests of cycads and tree ferns, ancient plants that were munched by dinosaurs. Page 39 describes some other greenery they ate.

When researching the dinosaur programmes I was stunned by an exciting revelation: dinosaurs aren't actually extinct! You can read the evidence for this on page 23. Most palaeontologists now agree that dinosaurs evolved into birds. Their skeletons are so similar that some fossil dinosaurs have been mistaken for birds and vice versa. So when you're immersed in the dinosaur world this book reveals, don't be too disappointed that they're long gone. Dinosaurs are still here right now, flying from tree to tree in your garden or local park.

Nigel Marven

Nigel Marven, naturalist and film-maker, wildlife consultant on ITV's *Prehistoric Park* and the BBC's *Walking with Dinosaurs* television specials

Skull of an *Edmontosaurus*, a duck-billed dinosaur that lived 71 to 65 million years ago

CHAPTER 1

World of dinosaurs

When we imagine a dinosaur, we usually picture a big animal – a massive plant-eater with a long neck, or a dragon-like meat-eater with sharp teeth and a fearsome temper. Such images are not wrong, but they do not tell the whole story. Since the discovery of dinosaurs nearly 200 years ago, our ideas about these prehistoric reptiles have kept changing. Every year, almost every week, fresh information comes to light. This new evidence includes fossilized remains as well as other clues about how dinosaurs lived and what sort of world they inhabited. Palaeontology, the study of ancient life, is a thriving science, and the study of fossil dinosaurs is an important part of this. Thanks to the work of palaeontologists, we now understand the world of dinosaurs better than ever before.

Argentinosaurus

Dinosaur families

Descended from a single ancestor, dinosaurs eventually evolved into more than 1,000 different species. Large or small, plant-eating or predatory, dinosaurs had many differences, but they also shared characteristics. Many walked on their toes, and they all had limbs that came straight down from their bodies rather than out from the sides, like those of many modern reptiles.

◄ Dinosaurs ranged in size from tiny predators to colossal plant-eaters. *Compsognathus*, a speedy hunter, weighed less than 3kg. At the other end of the scale, *Argentinosaurus* was a lumbering plant-eater, as tall as a four-storey building.

Great and small

Straight legs can support a heavy body better than bent legs. Just imagine if an elephant had legs that stuck out at the side like a lizard! Not only would it look silly, but it would not have the strength to lift its bulky body. Even the smallest dinosaurs had straight legs. Chicken-sized *Compsognathus* evolved from much bigger dinosaurs, and kept the straight legs of its ancestors.

Compsognathus

Dinosaur groups

Palaeontologists divide dinosaurs into two groups, based on their hip bones. These groups are the ornithischian (bird-hipped) dinosaurs and the saurischian (lizard-hipped) dinosaurs. The bird-hipped dinosaurs were all plant-eaters. Some were agile, two-legged runners, while others were slower-moving, armoured or plated dinosaurs. The lizard-hipped dinosaurs included meat-eaters as well as vegetarians. The terrifying carnivores *Tyrannosaurus rex* and *Allosaurus* were lizard-hipped dinosaurs.

Hips similar to those of modern lizards

Allosaurus

◀ Meat-eaters such as *Allosaurus* had quite small digestive systems. It was easy for them to walk on their hind legs. Eating plants requires a much bigger and more complex digestive system, so plant-eaters such as *Stegosaurus* were usually four-footed to support their heavy bodies.

▼ Lizard-hipped dinosaurs split into the meat-eating theropods and the long-necked, plant-eating sauropods. The bird-hipped dinosaurs were all plant-eaters. Some, such as the ornithopods, walked on two legs. Others went on four legs and carried varying arrangements of horns (ceratopsians), plates (stegosaurs) or armour (ankylosaurs). You can find out more about when these different dinosaur groups evolved in the timeline on page 59.

Stegosaurus

Hips similar to those of modern birds

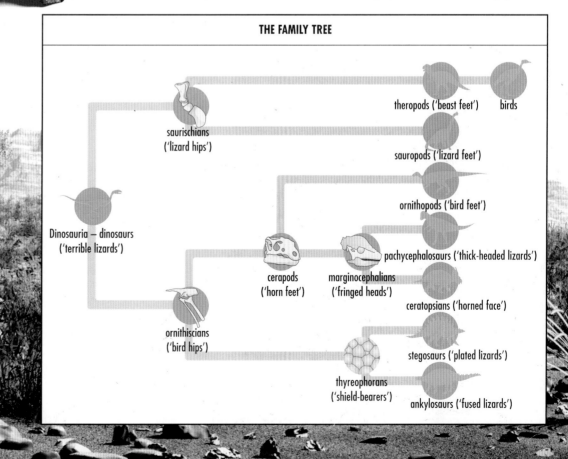

THE FAMILY TREE

saurischians ('lizard hips')

theropods ('beast feet')   birds

sauropods ('lizard feet')

Dinosauria – dinosaurs ('terrible lizards')

ornithopods ('bird feet')

pachycephalosaurs ('thick-headed lizards')

cerapods ('horn feet')

marginocephalians ('fringed heads')

ceratopsians ('horned face')

ornithiscians ('bird hips')

stegosaurs ('plated lizards')

thyreophorans ('shield-bearers')

ankylosaurs ('fused lizards')

Changing continents

The world of the earliest dinosaurs would have been unrecognizable to later species. When dinosaurs first appeared, there was just one big landmass on Earth. Over time, this split apart into the continents we know today. Unable to cross oceans, dinosaur populations became cut off and completely new species evolved. Asia's ceratopsian (or horned) dinosaurs, for example, looked very different from North America's famous *Triceratops*.

An island continent

During the Cretaceous period (145 to 65 million years ago, or mya), South America was like Australia is today – a massive continent completely surrounded by water. Also like Australia today, it had its own unique animal life, different from animal life anywhere else. The long-necked sauropods continued to be the main plant-eaters in South America after they had largely been replaced elsewhere by the duck-billed dinosaurs.

World on the move

How could continents move apart and break up? Earth's landmasses sit on large rafts of rock, called plates, that are constantly moving. Over millions of years, continents drift and oceans widen or close. This means that different time periods have very different physical geography and, as a result, very different climates, too.

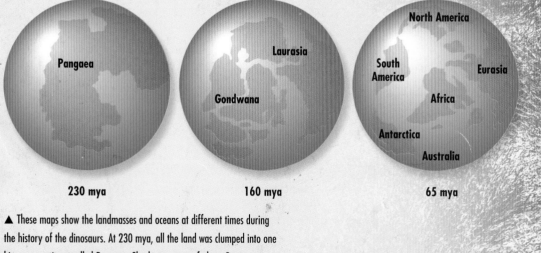

Pangaea

230 mya

Laurasia

Gondwana

160 mya

North America

South America

Eurasia

Africa

Antarctica

Australia

65 mya

▲ These maps show the landmasses and oceans at different times during the history of the dinosaurs. At 230 mya, all the land was clumped into one big supercontinent called Pangaea. Slowly, at a rate of about 2cm a year, Pangaea broke apart into the continents we know today. People who study how continents change are called palaeogeographers.

▼ *Triceratops* was a ceratopsian dinosaur that evolved in North America in the Cretaceous. Its name means 'three-horned face'. *Triceratops* lived alone or in family groups.

▲ The Triassic period lasted from 250 mya to 208 mya. The single Triassic continent had a hot, dry climate. The interior was so far from the ocean that it was uninhabitable desert. Life existed only around the edges, where the dominant plants were conifers and cycads.

▲ The Jurassic period lasted from 208 mya to 145 mya. During the Jurassic, the super-continent began to split up, creating flooded rift valleys. Shallow seas on the edge of the continent brought moister climates. Conifers, cycads, ferns and horsetails flourished.

▲ The Cretaceous period lasted from 145 mya to 65 mya. The Cretaceous saw the break-up of the supercontinent into smaller continents. Climates were warm and moist. Towards the end of the period, broad-leaved forests and flowering plants evolved.

Why dinosaurs died out

Dinosaurs ruled Earth for more than 165 million years but then, 65 million years ago, they suddenly disappeared. No one can be sure why this mass extinction took place, but there are many different theories. The most popular theory is that death came from outer space when a comet or a massive piece of rock, called a meteorite, crashed to Earth.

▶ A huge comet or meteorite strike would have killed everything in the immediate area, caused forest fires and sent tsunamis thundering across the oceans. The ash fallout could have lasted for centuries. The main evidence for this catastrophic event is a buried crater on the Yucatan Peninsula in Mexico that dates back to 65 million years ago.

Extraterrestrial impact

Many geologists believe that at the end of the Cretaceous Earth was hit by a comet or a 10km-wide meteorite. The impact created worldwide havoc, throwing up enough dust to blot out the Sun for decades. As evidence for this theory, scientists have found something unusual in rocks from 65 million years ago – they contain 100 times more iridium than they should. Iridium is a metal that is rare on the Earth's surface, but it is often found in space rock.

exposed KT boundary

▲ Whatever killed off the dinosaurs also made other life forms die out, including shellfish such as belemnites and this fossilized ammonite. Marine reptiles and pterosaurs disappeared. On land, every animal dog-sized or larger became extinct.

▲ Geologists look for clues about what happened at the end of the Cretaceous in rocks from that time. The KT boundary is the dividing line between rock laid down in the Cretaceous and rock from the next period, the Tertiary. It has been well studied in the badlands of Dakota, USA, where it has not been covered over by plants.

Other theories

An alternative explanation for the extinction is that volcanoes sent up the dust that blotted out the Sun. Volcanic activity was certainly intense at that time – northwest India is made up of lava that erupted at the end of the Cretaceous. This theory could also account for the iridium, brought up from the depths of the Earth. It is possible, of course, that both theories are right. Perhaps the volcanoes were somehow triggered by the impact of a comet or meteor.

▲ The dinosaurs may have become extinct at the end of the Cretaceous, but their descendants did not. These parrots are surviving theropods! All birds, from ducks to eagles, are direct descendants of the fierce meat-eaters of the Mesozoic era.

SUMMARY OF CHAPTER 1: WORLD OF DINOSAURS

What were the dinosaurs?

Dinosaurs were a group of ancient reptiles, distinguished by having a number of their backbones fused together between their hips. They stood more like a mammal than a modern reptile, with the legs swung beneath the body.

Kinds of dinosaurs

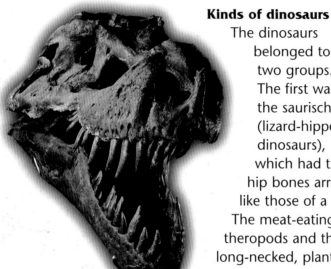

The dinosaurs belonged to two groups. The first was the saurischians (lizard-hipped dinosaurs), which had their hip bones arranged like those of a lizard. The meat-eating theropods and the long-necked, plant-eating sauropods were both lizard-hipped.

Tyrannosaurus rex skull

The second group was the ornithischians (bird-hipped dinosaurs), which had their hip bones arranged like those of a bird. All of the bird-hipped dinosaurs were plant-eaters, with complex chewing mechanisms and beaks at the front of their mouths. Bird-hipped dinosaurs included the two-legged ornithopods and various different types of dinosaurs that had armour.

Evidence of dinosaurs

The dinosaurs were extremely successful and existed for more than 165 million years. They spread out over the whole world at a time when the geography of the globe was changing. When they first appeared, all the landmasses were joined together as one supercontinent. By the time they disappeared, this had broken up into the individual continents that we know today. The dinosaurs all died out suddenly about 65 million years ago, probably as a result of a disaster such as a meteorite impact. We know about the dinosaurs because of their remains as fossils in rocks that formed at the time. Dinosaur fossils are rare, so our knowledge about them comes through in tiny trickles as new information appears.

Go further...

For general dinosaur information: www.enchantedlearning.com/subjects/dinosaurs/

See some of the best dinosaur artwork today: dino.lm.com

For dinosaur descriptions: www.dinodictionary.com

1001 Facts About Dinosaurs by Neil Clark and William Lindsay (Dorling Kindersley, 2002)

The Kingfisher Illustrated Dinosaur Encyclopedia by David Burnie (Kingfisher, 2001)

The Illustrated Encyclopedia of Dinosaurs by Dougal Dixon (Lorenz Books, 2006)

Climatologist
Studies climates – the average weather conditions and temperature of a place over a long period of time.

Geologist
Studies the composition of the Earth – the rocks and minerals that make it up, its history and the processes that act on it.

Palaeogeographer
Studies what the world was like in the very distant past – the positions of the continents and the conditions that existed on them.

Palaeontologist
Studies the fossilized remains of creatures that lived long ago.

See some of the first fossils at: The Natural History Museum, Cromwell Road, London SW7 5BD, UK
Telephone: +44 (0) 20 7942 5011
www.nhm.ac.uk

See a mounted *T rex* skeleton at: The Manchester Museum, University of Manchester, Oxford Road, Manchester M13 9PL
Telephone: +44 (0) 161 275 2648
www.manchester.ac.uk/museum

Visit the museum in Paris where fossil expert Baron Georges Cuvier worked: Musée National d'Histoire Naturelle, 57, rue Cuvier, 5th Arrondissement, Paris, France
Telephone: +33 (0) 1 40 79 56 01
www.mnhn.fr

Psittacosaurus, a dinosaur
with a parrot-like head that
lived in Asia in the Cretaceous

CHAPTER 2

Eurasia

Europe is the birthplace of dinosaur discovery. The first remains were found in England in the 1820s, and the name 'dinosaur' was coined in 1842 by British anatomist Sir Richard Owen while he was reporting on a scientific meeting. In those days, the remains were merely scraps of bone and teeth. The 1878 discovery of several dozen *Iguanodon* skeletons, many complete, in a mine in Bernissart, Belgium, gave the world its first view of what a complete dinosaur looked like. In Asia, teams from the American Museum of Natural History made spectacular finds in Mongolia's Gobi Desert, starting in the 1920s. More recently, in the last decade or so, there have been amazing discoveries in ancient lake deposits in Liaoning Province, China. These have included perfect skeletons of tiny dinosaurs and early birds.

The first dinosaur hunters

Imagine the thrill when people first discovered that giant
reptiles, many times larger than elephants, had once
roamed the Earth. The realization came in the 19th century.
Famous British fossil hunters included Mary Anning, William
Buckland and Gideon Mantell. Georges Cuvier was the
foremost expert in France. Edward Cope and Othniel
Marsh were important fossil hunters in the USA.

Coining a name

English anatomist Richard Owen (1804–1892) studied many
of the earliest fossil finds. To understand fossils he looked
at the anatomy of modern animals – he even dissected
a rhinoceros in his own living room! In 1842 Owen
came up with the name 'Dinosauria' ('terrible lizards')
to describe the group of extinct land reptiles.

The big lizard

The first dinosaur species to be named
was *Megalosaurus*, meaning 'big lizard'.
British professor William Buckland
(1784–1856) had found a fossil of its
broken jaw in a quarry near Stonesfield, a
short horse ride away from Oxford. Buckland
presented the specimen at a scientific meeting
in London on 20 February 1824.

▲ *Megalosaurus* fossils have been found in England,
France and Portugal, but never a whole skeleton. The
fossilized jaw found by William Buckland showed new
teeth growing up to replace old ones. As a meat-eater,
Megalosaurus may have lost teeth as it bit into prey.

jawbone

◄ Quarries were excellent searching grounds for early
hunters. In the early 1820s, an English doctor called Gideon
Mantell (1790–1852) made a great discovery at this quarry near
Cuckfield in southern England. He and his wife Mary found
fossilized bones and teeth belonging to the dinosaur *Iguanodon*.

The fossil record

Experts estimate that less than one per cent of all dinosaurs were preserved as fossils. It is very rare for fossils to be found by accident. More often, they are discovered as a result of dedicated teamwork – and months of painstaking effort. But there is always an element of luck!

Finding and mapping sites

In the early days of a dig, field geologists go prospecting – surveying for rocks that are likely to be rich in fossils. Once the site has been chosen, the hard work of clearing and digging begins. Most teams include student volunteers as well as professional scientists. Some team members may have special responsibility for running a field website, uploading images and diaries.

Excavating the fossil

Fossil bones are fragile. When they are still partly encased in rock, the palaeontologists cover them with bandages dipped in plaster of Paris. This protects the bones from breaking. Back in the laboratory, the plaster jacket is cut away, and preparators reveal the fossil bit by bit. Microscopes and 3-D X-rays called CAT scans allow an even closer look.

▶ A 70-million-year-old fossil is uncovered in the Gobi Desert, Mongolia. The original picture of the dig site has been altered here to show what the fossil eventually looked like after being cleaned and prepared in the laboratory. The bones belong to an *Oviraptor* that died defending its nest of 22 eggs.

MEET THE EXPERT: DAVID VARRICCHIO

American palaeontologist David Varricchio visited a site in the Gobi Desert in 2001. His job was to describe its geology. Rocks reveal what the whole environment was like millions of years ago, and what event caused animals to be buried there.

DIG-SITE TOOLS

A tape measure and plumb bob are essential for mapping and plotting. The plumb bob shows when lines are straight.

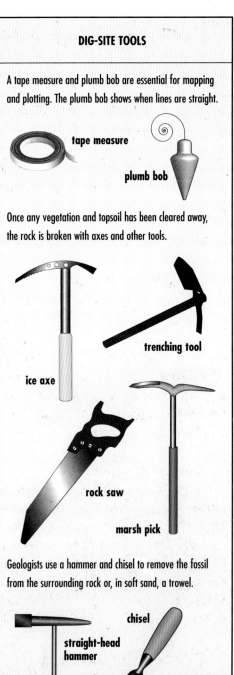

tape measure

plumb bob

Once any vegetation and topsoil has been cleared away, the rock is broken with axes and other tools.

trenching tool

ice axe

rock saw

marsh pick

Geologists use a hammer and chisel to remove the fossil from the surrounding rock or, in soft sand, a trowel.

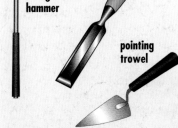

chisel

straight-head hammer

pointing trowel

Brushes and dental picks are used for close, delicate work, brushing or scraping away any sediment.

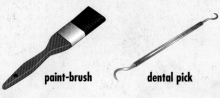

paint-brush

dental pick

Fighting dinosaurs

Mark Norell of the American Museum of Natural History has a special interest in the fighting dinosaurs fossil. In 2000, he commissioned computer animators to bring the dinosaur duel to life for a special exhibition of the fossil. He has also worked to show how theropods such as *Velociraptor* had feathers, not scales.

The Gobi Desert in Mongolia has been a rich source of fossils ever since the first *Protoceratops* skull was found there by Roy Chapman Andrews in 1922. A fossil known as the 'fighting dinosaurs' was discovered there in 1971. It shows a *Protoceratops* and *Velociraptor* locked in a fight to the death. They were buried alive 80 million years ago, during a landslide.

Victim and attacker

Protoceratops was a plant-eater that had a bony shield to protect its neck. Although it belonged to the ceratopsian (horned dinosaur) family, it did not have horns – just bony lumps and bumps on its face. Its main defence was running away, and it had broad, hoof-like claws that could dig into the sandy ground. *Velociraptor* was *Protoceratops*' chief enemy. This predator had slender but powerful jaws that contained long rows of bladed teeth. It also had massive claws, which it used to grip its prey.

▶ The Mongolian dinosaurs were fairly small – the meat-eaters were about the size of large dogs and the herbivores were sheep-sized. *Protoceratops* was so common that it is sometimes called 'the sheep of the Cretaceous'.

◀ This animatronic model of a feathered *Velociraptor* was built for London's Natural History Museum. Plumage would have kept in body heat — essential for an active, warm-blooded hunter. The feathers may have been brightly coloured for display, or dull for camouflage. They certainly were not used for flying.

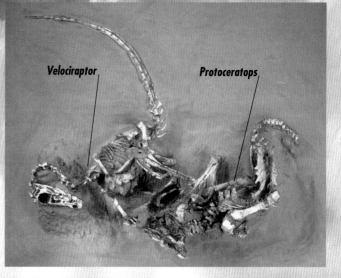

Velociraptor   **Protoceratops**

▲ The famous fighting dinosaurs fossil captures two dinosaurs in an embrace of death. The *Velociraptor* has grasped its victim's head in its clawed hands and embedded its feet deep in the plant-eater's belly. *Protoceratops* is fighting back, snapping its enemy's arm tightly in its beak.

Gobi treasure trove

American fossil hunter Roy Chapman Andrews (1884–1960) described his 1922 fossil hunt to the Gobi Desert as 'the biggest land scientific expedition ever to leave the United States'. His extraordinary finds included skeletons of adult and juvenile *Protoceratops*, as well as the *Velociraptor*s that preyed upon them. Later expeditions to the area uncovered hundreds of dinosaur eggs. Some had been laid by *Protoceratops*, while others belonged to *Oviraptor*. The name *Oviraptor* means 'egg thief'. When *Oviraptor* was first discovered, palaeontologists did not know that all dinosaurs laid eggs. They thought that *Oviraptor* must have stolen *Protoceratops*' eggs.

Feathered dinosaurs

Until the 1990s, all dinosaurs were thought to have scaly, reptilian skin. The only question was what colour the skin was, as fossilization does not preserve colour. Then, in 1995, the first feathered dinosaur, *Sinosauropteryx*, was discovered in China. Feathers may have first appeared when reptile scales frayed at the edges and became downy fluff, which kept dinosaurs warm. Later, fluff evolved into feathers, perhaps for display.

MEET THE EXPERT: XU XING

Palaeontologist Xu Xing has found more than 25 dinosaurs and discovered much evidence that birds are dinosaurs. His spectacular specimens include small meat-eating dinosaurs with feathers, not scales. Xing works in Liaoning Province, China. Around 130 million years ago, volcanic eruptions in the region preserved Early Cretaceous animals in a layer of ash.

▶ A pair of *Microraptor*s flash their feathers, perhaps to fight for territory or to attract a mate. *Microraptor* was about the size of a crow, and probably not capable of powered flight. However, it could have spread its wings to glide from tree to tree.

▲ The very fine fossil of *Microraptor* clearly shows the feathers fanning out from the arms and the legs. These limbs evidently formed two pairs of wings. The feathered tail would have provided steering as *Microraptor* glided through Cretaceous skies.

Wings outstretched
for gliding

Showy tail feathers

Downy
body covering

How flight began

Most palaeontologists agree that birds evolved
from dinosaurs. However they do not agree on how
flight evolved. Some believe that it was a 'trees-down'
process, in which a climbing animal learned to glide from
branches. This helped it move from tree to tree. Others
believe in a 'ground-up' process, in which a running and
jumping animal evolved wings that helped it to run faster
and jump higher – so that it could be better at hunting
insects and other small, speedy prey.

From dromaeosaurs to birds

The fast little hunters called dromaeosaurs were the
most bird-like of the dinosaurs. Their limbs were hollow,
and they were probably warm-blooded and covered
in feathers for insulation. They must be birds' closest
relatives. However, they appeared later than the first birds,
showing that the evolutionary line is quite complex. It has
even been suggested that dromaeosaurs were actually
early birds that had lost their powers of flight!

FEATHERED DINOSAURS

Sinosauropteryx was very similar
to the tiny *Compsognathus*, but it
was covered in a fine covering of
downy feathers. It must have had
an active lifestyle.

Protarchaeopteryx had bunches
of long feathers on its tail and
wings. Despite its 'wings',
Protarchaeopteryx could not fly.

Mei was found curled up like
a sleeping duck, with its head
tucked under its arm. Its full
scientific name – *Mei long* –
means 'sleeping dragon'.

Flying reptiles

Pterosaurs, the first backboned creatures to fly, appeared in the Late Triassic and soared over the heads of the dinosaurs. From the Late Jurassic, they shared the skies with early birds. Pterosaurs had a variety of feeding techniques. Some snapped up insects in mid-air, others swooped down to scoop up fish and some may have even scavenged dinosaur carcasses.

Little and large

Pterosaurs came in many shapes and sizes. The earliest ones had long tails but the pterodactyls, which came later, had short, stumpy tails. Some pterosaurs were barely bigger than blackbirds, while others were the size of small aircraft. Unlike birds, whose wings are made of feathers, pterosaurs had wings of living tissue, containing a network of blood vessels. Pterosaurs were warm-blooded and had a fine covering of hair to conserve their body heat.

◀ Gliding reptiles appeared more than 260 mya — way before the pterosaurs — but they could not stay airborne for long. *Xianglong*, a gliding lizard that lived 125 mya, looked very like this modern *Draco* lizard from Southeast Asia.

▶ This Late Jurassic scene shows pterosaurs flying, feeding and nesting. The best pterosaur fossils are of species that lived near water. That is because their remains ended up on the seabed and, over time, became preserved as sedimentary rock formed.

► The earliest known bird, *Archaeopteryx*, is known from about eight specimens. The best are so detailed that we can see the feathers of the wings and tail, and we can tell how the arrangement of the wing feathers is identical to that of modern birds.

PTEROSAUR JAWS

Istiodactylus (which used to be known as *Ornithodesmus*) had a wide, duck-like jaw filled with sharp teeth. It probably fed on fish. Its wingspan was 5m – longer than a car.

Dsungaripterus had an upturned jaw with a pointy tip – a perfect shape for poking into rocky crevices. *Dsungaripterus* could have winkled out crabs and shellfish, then crushed them in its teeth.

Pteranodon was one of the largest pterosaurs, with toothless jaws that were 1.2m long, twice as long as a man's arm. Skimming low over the sea, it scooped up mouthfuls of fish.

Pterodaustro had the oddest jaw of all. It was packed with around 500 elastic bristles, each about 4cm long, which it used for sieving small creatures from the shallow water.

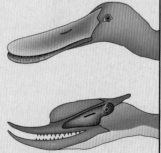

Early bird

Archaeopteryx evolved from a small dinosaur. Its fossils show that it had dinosaur-like jaws and teeth, dinosaur-like claws on the forelimbs and a dinosaur-like bony tail. Pterosaurs also had these features, but their wings were quite different and evolved independently. The birds lived alongside the pterosaurs, and when these flying reptiles perished with the dinosaurs, the birds became the rulers of the skies.

Marine reptiles

Before anybody knew about dinosaurs, the study of ancient sea reptiles was well under way. Fossils of sea animals are far more common than those of land animals. This is because most fossils are preserved in sedimentary rock, which forms when sediment piles up at the bottom of the sea. In the late 18th and early 19th centuries, geologists and anatomists were studying the strange animals that swam in the ancient oceans.

MARINE REPTILE GROUPS

Nothosaurs (245–228 mya) had webbed feet or flippers. They hunted in shallow coastal waters.

Pliosaurs (200–65 mya) had compact bodies, short necks, massive heads and ferocious jaws.

Mosasaurs (140–65 mya) swam by rippling their bodies, using their flippers only for steering and stability.

Ichthyosaurs (247–140 mya) had four flippers, crescent-shaped tails and streamlined, dolphin-like bodies.

Plesiosaurs (200–65 mya) had four broad flippers, or paddles. They swung their necks through shoals of fish.

Shelled reptiles included placodonts (240–200 mya) and turtles (215 mya to the present day).

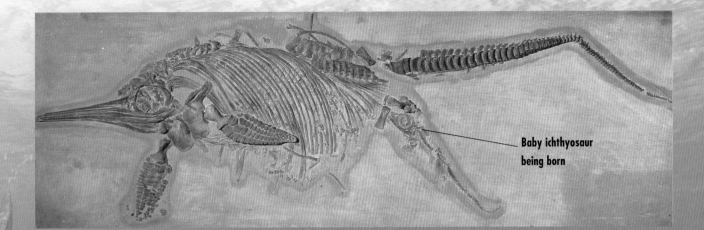

Baby ichthyosaur being born

▲ Ichthyosaurs were superbly adapted for life at sea. Unlike other marine reptiles, they did not come ashore to lay eggs. Instead, they had live young out in the ocean. This *Ichthyosaurus* specimen was fossilized in the act of giving birth.

▲ *Plesiosaurus* used its large paddles to power through the water after prey. It waved its long, flexible neck this way and that, picking off fish from a shoal. *Plesiosaurus* grew only to about 3m, but one of its relatives, *Elasmosaurus*, grew as long as 14m.

Underwater flight

Plesiosaurs, and their short-necked, big-headed relatives the pliosaurs, swam through the water in a kind of flying motion. The legs had evolved into stiff paddles, reinforced by a mosaic of bones that had once formed the fingers and wrists. These paddles worked rather like the wings of a bird. By flapping them slowly up and down, the animal moved forwards. Modern-day turtles, penguins and sea lions move through the water with a similar action.

Swimming and hunting

The ichthyosaurs and mosasaurs swam with a rippling motion of the body and tail, using their paddle legs for steering. Mosasaurs were like giant swimming lizards – the largest grew to 17m. They ate just about anything, from ammonites to sharks and plesiosaurs. Ichthyosaurs fed on squid-like shellfish called belemnites. Some had eyes as large as dinner plates, so they could dive to deep, dark depths in search of prey.

SUMMARY OF CHAPTER 2: EURASIA

Early studies
Europe is where the systematic study of fossil vertebrates (backboned animals) first started. In the late 18th and early 19th centuries, the bones of mosasaurs, plesiosaurs and ichthyosaurs were being recognized for what they were – the remains of ancient animals. These prehistoric marine reptiles were collected and studied scientifically. In dinosaur times, much of Europe was covered in shallow seas, in which these animals lived.

Land reptiles
The study expanded to include ancient land reptiles following three key discoveries – William Buckland's *Megalosaurus*, found in 1822, and the two specimens identified by Gideon Mantell, *Iguanodon*, found in 1825, and the armoured *Hylaeosaurus*, found in 1832. Richard Owen established the classification (biological group) of Dinosauria to accommodate these three new animals.

The science spreads
In the 20th and 21st centuries there have been finds all across Europe and Asia. The Cretaceous rocks of the Gobi Desert have been studied since the 1920s. Here scientists have found the fossils of early horned dinosaurs and small, fast meat-eaters. Fossilized dinosaur eggs have also been found in the Gobi, along with the parents that died trying to brood them. Further east, in China, there are ancient lake deposits that have fossils of early birds and tiny feathered dinosaurs. The smallest dinosaurs that ever lived are turning up there.

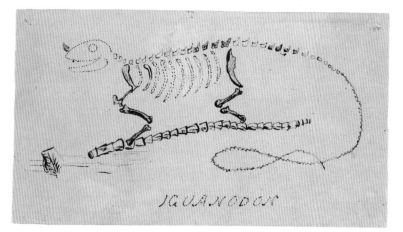

Drawing of *Iguanodon* by Gideon Mantell

Go further...

Follow up some of the best TV programmes on dinosaurs: www.bbc.co.uk /sn/prehistoric_life

Read a thorough overview of the subject of dinosaurs: www.ucmp.berkeley.edu/diapsids/ dinosaur.html

Read about Gideon Mantell and his discovery of *Iguanodon*: www.strange science.net/mantell.htm

Dinosaur Quest by John Sibbick and Steve Parker (Ian Grant Publishers, 2005)

Feathered Dinosaurs of China by Gregory Wenzel (Charlesbridge Publishing, 2004)

Anatomist
Studies how animals are built and what the different parts of their bodies are used for.

Field geologist
Goes out and works on rock outcrops ('out in the field') rather than just studying rocks in the laboratory.

Naturalist
Studies nature and living things, especially animals and plants.

Ornithologist
Studies birds. Some ornithologists observe birds out in the wild, or use technologies such as radar to track populations. Others study bird anatomy in the laboratory.

See how 19th-century scientists thought dinosaurs looked, as life-sized statues in the grounds of: Crystal Palace Park, Thicket Road, Penge, London SE20 8DT, UK Telephone +44 (0) 20 8778 9496 www.crystalpalacefoundation.org.uk

Visit displays of the dinosaurs from the Gobi in: American Museum of Natural History, Central Park West and 79th Street, New York City, USA Telephone +1 212 769 5100 www.amnh.org

'Feathered Dinosaurs of China' is a travelling exhibit that has been touring many museums worldwide since 2002. Check if it comes to your local area.

CHAPTER 3

The Americas

After Europe, North America was the next place for dinosaur discoveries. In the second half of the 19th century, dinosaur hunters pressed westwards, finding fossilized bones as they went. Two professors – Edward Cope of Pennsylvania and Othniel Marsh of Yale – became bitter rivals as they tried to outdo one another in the number of their finds. Dinomania spread. Around 150 types of dinosaur had been discovered by 1900. Canada became the next important hunting area, with dinosaurs even being found as far north as Alaska. Starting in the 1970s, South America became a dinosaur hunter's paradise. The vast plains of Argentina have thrown up all kinds of dinosaurs and even nesting sites, while areas of Brazil are now famous for their pterosaurs and fish-eating dinosaurs.

Exposed sauropod backbones on the quarry wall at Dinosaur National Monument, Utah, USA

Hunting in packs

During the Cretaceous period, North America was home to some terrifying predators. Dromaeosaurs such as *Dromaeosaurus* and *Deinonychus* were intelligent and fast-moving, often working together in packs to bring down creatures much larger than themselves. They shared their habitat with other brainy hunters, such as *Troodon* and the ornithomimids ('bird mimics').

Killing machine

Imagine a hunting dinosaur the size of a wolf. Give it long hind legs and the running speed of a greyhound. Equip each foot with a huge, curved claw that could hook into flesh. Make it as intelligent as a bird of prey. You have imagined a dromaeosaur.

▲ A pack of wolf-sized *Deinonychus* attacks a *Tenontosaurus*. Curved claws on their fingers and a massive, sickle-shaped claw on their second toe allow them to hook on to their victim. They bite and bite again, slashing the *Tenontosaurus* with razor-sharp teeth until it finally collapses from loss of blood.

▲ Like the dromaeosaurs, *Troodon* was armed with lethal claws. It also had a relatively large brain, making it one of the smartest dinosaurs around. It had large eyes, so it possibly hunted at dusk or at night.

MEET THE EXPERT: PHIL MANNING

Palaeontologist Phil Manning demonstrated that dromaeosaurs could not have used their outsize claws to kill. He attached a life-size *Deinonychus* claw to a robotic arm and thrust it into a slab of meat. It did not go in deeply enough to have caused fatal wounds. Manning realized that the claws were not for wounding, but for hooking on to prey before biting it to death.

The gentle relative

The ornithomimids were a group of fast-running dinosaurs. The name, meaning 'bird mimic', comes from their resemblance to modern ostriches. Ornithomimids used their speed for escape rather than for hunting. Instead of jaws full of deadly teeth, they had a toothless beak. Bird mimics probably fed on small animals such as lizards, mammals and insects. Some of them may even have been fruit-eaters.

◀ *Struthiomimus* (the 'ostrich mimic') was one of the ornithomimids. Its muscular legs helped to carry it away from dangerous dromaeosaurs. It had a short, light tail and could run at speeds of 50km/h – as fast as a racehorse.

Armoured dinosaurs

Early plant-eaters relied on size to protect them from predators. Later, some herbivores evolved body armour. Ceratopsians, or horned dinosaurs, were the tanks of the dinosaur world. Like rhinos today, they had fearsome horns. Nodosaurs and ankylosaurs had all-over armour, with horns, bony plates and, sometimes, a tail weapon.

Horned dinosaurs

Ceratopsians ranged across the northern hemisphere. *Triceratops*, *Styracosaurus* and *Centrosaurus* inhabited what is now North America. Many of these plant-eaters had powerful beaks that could snap through branches. However, their main features were their formidable horns, which projected from bony skull shields, edged with a frill of spikes. The biggest ceratopsians were a match for any predator, including *Tyrannosaurus rex*.

Bony armour and plates

The armoured dinosaurs were common at the end of the Cretaceous period, mostly on the northern continents, although one fossil has been found in Australia. There were two types. The first were the nodosaurs, which had armoured backs and spikes along the sides, especially on the shoulders. The ankylosaurs had no side spikes but a bony club on the end of the tail.

▲ *Euoplocephalus* was a typical armoured ankylosaur. Even its eyelids were armoured — they protected the eyes like steel shutters. *Euoplocephalus* had a tail club, too, for striking back at predators.

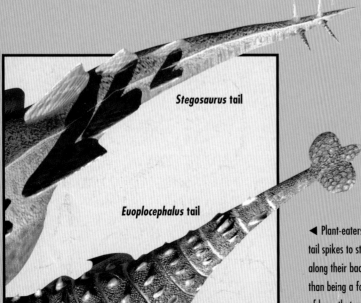

Stegosaurus tail

Euoplocephalus tail

◄ Plant-eaters' tails were formidable weapons. Stegosaurs had tail spikes to stab attackers. They also had bony plates or spines along their back, but these were probably for heat loss, rather than being a form of armour. *Euoplocephalus* had a club-like knob of bone that could break a predator's leg with a single swipe.

► This fossilized skull belongs to *Triceratops*. Like all ceratopsians, it had a heavy head and an armoured shield around its neck. In some species, this shield was ringed with spikes. *Triceratops* had three horns on its head. Other ceratopsians had two, one or even none.

Famous giants

Patagonia, in Argentina, is a hot spot for dinosaur bones. For tens of millions of years, the region was a humid swamp inhabited by dinosaurs. Around 130 million years ago it was home to *Amargasaurus*, a 9m-long beast with forked spines down its back. From 100 to 80 million years ago, Patagonia was a land of giants. Herds of colossal *Argentinosaurus* were stalked by terrifying predators, which were possibly bigger than *Tyrannosaurus rex*.

Giant sauropod

Argentinosaurus ('Argentina lizard') was possibly the largest, heaviest land animal that has ever lived. From the bones they have, experts estimate that *Argentinosaurus* was 35m long and weighed more than 15 elephants. It was one of the specialized sauropods that survived on the island continent of South America even after sauropods had begun to disappear elsewhere. Cretaceous South America had been isolated for so long that animals continued to evolve there that were found nowhere else.

▲ With average rainfall of around 130mm per year, Patagonia has an extremely dry climate. There is very little vegetation, so rocks lie exposed in the dusty desert. Any fossils contained within the rocks, such as this dinosaur spine, are easily seen.

▲ The middle vertebra (backbone segment) in this picture belonged to *Argentinosaurus*, while the two on either side came from smaller sauropods. The wide parts of the bones anchored powerful muscles and cable-like ligaments (bundles of tissue). In life, these were needed to support and power the huge body.

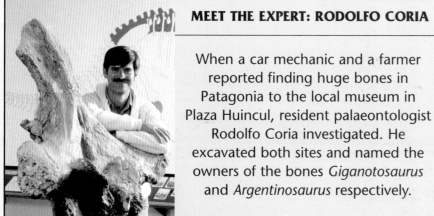
▼ A *Giganotosaurus* brings down a young *Argentinosaurus*. To take on an adult sauropod, *Giganotosaurus* had to work as part of a team. In this reconstruction, *Buitreraptors* lurk in the background, ready to dart in for scraps of meat. These scavengers behaved like jackals at a lion kill today.

Giant theropod

For decades we regarded *Tyrannosaurus rex* as the largest, fiercest dinosaur that ever lived. Nowadays, however, we are finding the remains of even bigger meat-eaters, such as *Giganotosaurus* from the Middle Cretaceous of South America. Like all theropods, *Giganotosaurus* had a huge head, sharp teeth and clawed hands that it held out at the front, balanced by a heavy tail. It probably preyed on the huge sauropods of the time. It was more closely related to the earlier allosaurs than the later tyrannosaurs.

Hell Creek today

H ell Creek! What an exciting-sounding name!
For palaeontologists, this bleak badland area in the
remote Midwest, USA, more than lives up to its name.
Sixty-five million years ago it was the stomping ground
of *Tyrannosaurus rex*, *Triceratops* and many other famous
dinosaurs. Today, its rocks are revealing some of the most
impressive dinosaur fossils that have ever been found.

Hell's inhabitants

The sandstones of Hell Creek were deposited in rivers
and swamps over a period of 2 million years, at the very
end of the Cretaceous period. There are fossils of laurels,
magnolias and conifers – the remains of ancient forests.
Among these plant fossils, palaeontologists are finding the
bones of duck-billed dinosaurs and ceratopsians. There is
also evidence of small meat-eaters, such as dromaeosaurs
and *Troodon*, as well as the mighty *Tyrannosaurus rex*.

▲ A trackway discovered by Phil Manning in the Hell Creek rocks
may show the first known footprints of *Tyrannosaurus*. The shape
and the size are right, and *Tyrannosaurus* lived in the area at that
time. However, without any other evidence, ichnologists (fossil
footprint experts) cannot definitely say what made the tracks.

▼ A fossil hunter walks
through the dusty Dakota
badlands. Over many
thousands of years, wind,
rain and ice have worn away
the landscape. The weathering
has exposed layers of Hell
Creek Formation rock, which
are rich in dinosaur fossils.

Crooked
Creek
Formation

Hell Creek Bay

Fort Peck Lake

Peterson
Point

Hell Creek
Formation

MONTANA

North
America

▲ The Hell Creek Formation is named after exposed sections
of Cretaceous rock that run along Hell Creek in Montana, USA.
However, the rock formation – and its prehistoric treasure –
is spread over parts of North and South Dakota, too.

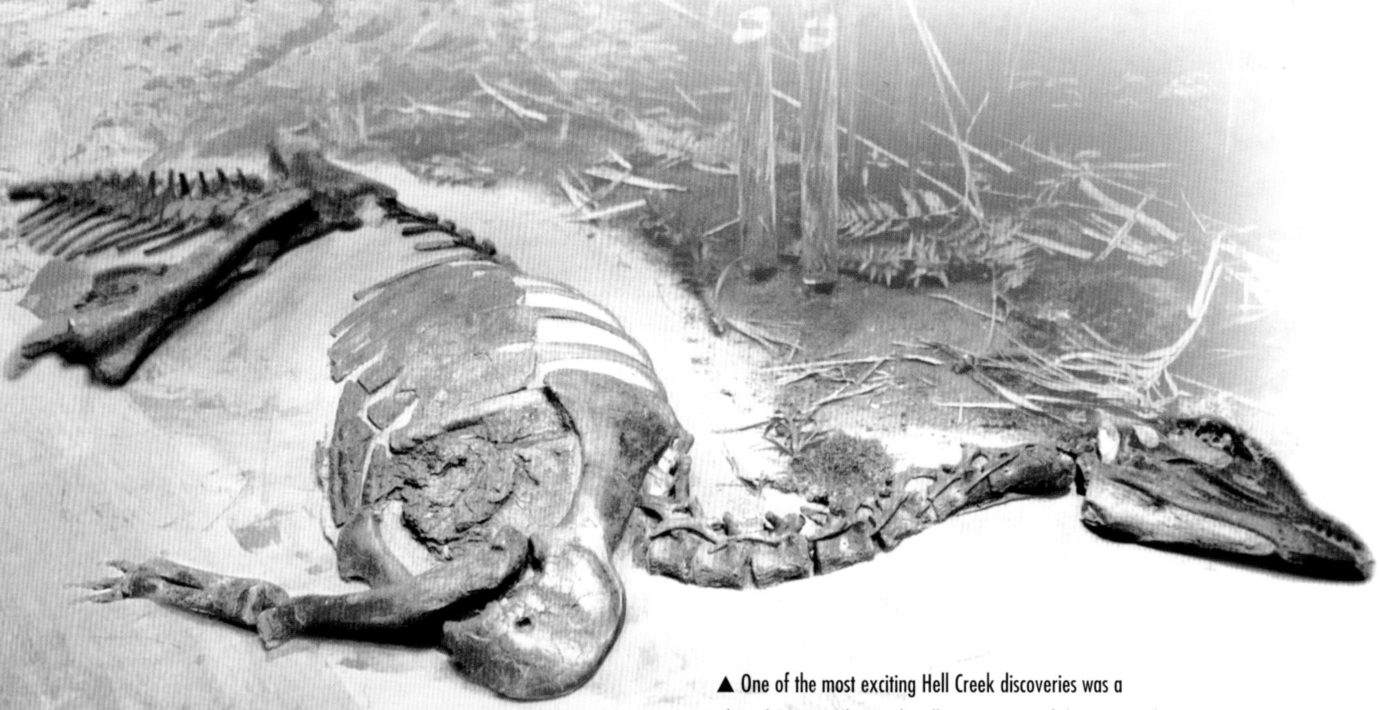

▲ One of the most exciting Hell Creek discoveries was a *Thescelosaurus* nicknamed 'Willow'. Remains of this cow-sized herbivore had been found before, but Willow was special because preserved inside its chest were the remains of a structure that some have interpreted as a heart (see page 45).

Tyrant king

Tyrannosaurus had a massive skull, with teeth and jaws that were powerful enough to crush bone. Its eyes were able to focus forwards on its prey. Its body weighed as much as an elephant, but this terrifying meat-eater was still able to race along on its mighty hind legs. What a monster! No wonder the scientists gave it a name that means 'king of the tyrant reptiles'.

◀ More than 50 *Tyrannosaurus* specimens have been discovered since the first one was found in 1905. The skeleton shown here is one of the most complete *Tyrannosaurus*. It was nicknamed 'Stan' after its finder, Stan Sacrison. It is now mounted in the Black Hills Museum in Hill City, South Dakota, USA.

Hell Creek long ago

Imagine dinosaurs lumbering through the Everglades, a 21st-century swamp on the coast of Florida, USA, and you get a good idea of what prehistoric Hell Creek was like. The climate was hot, damp and perfect for dinosaurs. There were many kinds of insects, including dragonflies and bloodsucking mosquitoes. The dinosaurs there would also have been hearing bird calls, just as we do today.

Animals of Hell Creek
With its lush, forested riverbanks and steamy swamps, Hell Creek had a thriving ecosystem 65 million years ago. The forest trees and undergrowth were browsed by plant-eating dinosaurs such as ceratopsians and duckbills. These, in turn, were hunted by the big meat-eaters. Smaller animals such as turtles and birds were hunted by the smaller meat-eating dinosaurs and by crocodiles.

KEY

1. TRICERATOPS

The biggest of the horned ceratopsians, with three horns and an armoured shield. It probably ate only certain kinds of plant.

2. TYRANNOSAURUS

The biggest and fiercest meat-eating dinosaur of the time. It probably hunted the duckbills and fought the ceratopsians.

3. BRACHYCHAMPSA

One of the many types of crocodile that infested the rivers. In appearance it was very much like a modern crocodile.

4. EDMONTOSAURUS

One of the duck-billed dinosaurs that roamed the area in herds. With its broad, duck-like beak, it ate almost any kind of plant.

5. AVISAURUS

A bird of prey that resembled an eagle, although it was not related. It hunted the smaller animals of the area.

6. HELOPANOPLIA

A water-living turtle that looked and behaved very much like its modern relative – the soft-shelled, freshwater turtle, *Trionyx*.

Vegetation at Hell Creek

Plant life was changing in the Late Cretaceous. There were still many conifers, but the ancient cycads and gingkoes were on the way out. A new group of plants was taking over – plants with flowers. Vegetation was no longer just green. Flowers had colour to attract pollinating insects. Grasses did not evolve until after the extinction of the dinosaurs, but the Hell Creek landscape may have included some trees still around today, such as birch, beech, figs, palms, oak and willow.

Hadrosaurs

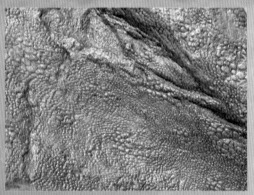

▲ This specimen of fossilized skin found in Wyoming, USA, belonged to *Edmontosaurus*, one of the largest hadrosaurs. It shows that the dinosaur had raised nodules on its skin. Fossilized skin is rare. It formed only when hot, dry conditions mummified a dead dinosaur and prevented its soft tissues from rotting.

With flattened snouts that resembled ducks' beaks, hadrosaurs are sometimes nicknamed duck-billed dinosaurs. They were mid-sized dinosaurs, between 6m and 18m long, and they usually lived in herds. They are most famous for their flamboyant heads, since many hadrosaurs had hollow crests in unusual shapes. Their jaws were distinctive, too, containing multiple rows of hundreds of teeth for chewing tough vegetation.

▼ *Parasaurolophus* had a crest up to 1.8m long – the most impressive of any hadrosaur. Here, a *Parasaurolophus* group comes to the river to drink, unaware that a 15m-long crocodile, *Deinosuchus*, is lying in wait to ambush one of them.

▶ This is a model *Maiasaura* nest. The real thing consisted of a mound of soil, about 1m high and 2m wide, with a hollow in the top. *Maiasaura* herds nested together, with each nest within pecking distance of the next.

Good mothers

In the 1970s, palaeontologist Jack Horner found a nesting site in Montana belonging to a new species of hadrosaur. Horner called the 10m-long creature *Maiasaura* ('good mother lizard'), because it seemed that the parents cared for their young, feeding them berries, seeds and leaves. Some nests had newly-hatched babies, just 50cm long, while others contained older ones, as long as 2m.

Making music

The duckbill's crest was probably used for making a noise. A long, tubular crest like that of *Parasaurolophus* would have made a noise like a trombone. Smaller crests created different sounds. The calls were used for communication and keeping the herd together.

Titanosaur nursery

In 1997 an extraordinary nesting site was discovered in Patagonia, Argentina. From the fossilized remains, we can imagine the scene 80 million years ago. Female *Saltasaurus* dinosaurs, each weighing 7 tonnes, gathered on a flood plain to lay their eggs. Each female dug a shallow nest, flicking sand and soil into the air, then dropped in its eggs with a soft plop. After laying as many as 30 eggs, the female covered the nest with earth and left the eggs to be hatched by the warmth of the sun.

▲ There is no evidence that any adult *Saltasaurus* remained to guard the nesting site. Most eggs and hatchlings would have been picked off by predatory *Aucasaurus* dinosaurs. Hatchlings would have begun feeding immediately – it would take 15 or 20 years for them to reach their adult size.

MEET THE EXPERT: LUIS CHIAPPÉ

Argentinian palaeontologist Luis Chiappé led the team that discovered the *Saltasaurus* nursery. He was looking for fossilized birds, not dinosaur eggs! Instead, Chiappé stumbled upon the world's biggest dinosaur nesting site and the first-ever discovery of sauropod embryos. The site was in a region of Patagonia called Auca Mahuida. Chiappé's team renamed it 'Auca Mahuevo', playing on the Spanish word *huevo*, meaning 'egg'.

Regular nesting

We cannot tell how often the *Saltasaurus* herds visited Auca Mahuevo, or for how long the nesting site was in operation. However, the thickness of the sediments suggest that it was probably a regular nesting area for hundreds of years.

Dead eggs

We know about the nesting site because once in a while it was flooded by a nearby river. This buried the eggs in mud, and they fossilized. Most of the time, however, this did not happen and the eggs that were not eaten hatched safely. The youngsters left the site and the eggshells rotted away, leaving no sign that they had ever been there.

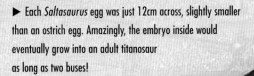

► Each *Saltasaurus* egg was just 12cm across, slightly smaller than an ostrich egg. Amazingly, the embryo inside would eventually grow into an adult titanosaur as long as two buses!

Warm- or cold-blooded?

For a long time, palaeontologists thought that dinosaurs were cold-blooded, like modern reptiles. Cold-blooded animals cannot produce their own heat. Their temperature changes depending on their surroundings. However, since the late 1960s, some palaeontologists have argued that dinosaurs could have been warm-blooded, like mammals and birds today. Warm-blooded animals are able to keep their bodies at a constant temperature.

▼ A constant body temperature would have been useful to a speedy hunter such as this *Bambiraptor*. If *Bambiraptor* was warm-blooded, it would have needed an efficient, chambered heart to pump blood upwards to its head.

Cold-blooded reptiles

A cold-blooded animal's metabolism (how it makes energy from food) requires less food than a warm-blooded animal's. So a cold-blooded dinosaur would have hunted in violent spurts of activity, with long rests in-between. Some experts say that a big meat-eater such as *Tyrannosaurus* would never have been able to hunt enough food if it were warm-blooded, so it must have been cold-blooded.

◄ One theory suggests that the biggest dinosaurs, such as *Diplodocus*, were so massive that they held on to their warmth, instead of cooling as the weather cooled. This is known as being gigantothermic. By retaining heat, they could have had a warm-blooded lifestyle without needing a warm-blooded metabolism.

► Fossilized dinosaur hearts are extremely rare. Experts are divided on whether this fossil, discovered in South Dakota, is a heart at all. Certainly no-one has found a heart yet in a good enough state for the chambers inside to be counted. When we examine animals that are alive today, we see that warm-blooded ones need four-chambered hearts but cold-blooded ones only need three-chambered hearts.

Dark ring inside *Thescelosaurus* chest cavity has been interpreted as a heart

► A warm-blooded predator needs about ten times as much food as a cold-blooded one — so 100 antelope could feed one lion for a year, or ten crocodiles. Palaeontologists can compare the numbers of predators and prey to guess whether dinosaurs were warm- or cold-blooded. There are relatively few predatory dinosaur fossils compared to those of plant-eaters, which could be evidence that the predators were warm-blooded.

Different metabolisms

A warm-blooded dinosaur could hunt at any time of the day or night, and in any climate. Perhaps, though, terms such as cold-blooded and warm-blooded are too fixed. It might be more helpful to think of the active, meat-eating dinosaurs as closer to being warm-blooded and the big plant-eaters as closer to being cold-blooded.

SUMMARY OF CHAPTER 3: THE AMERICAS

Dinosaur societies

The finds of North and South America have given us plenty of insight into dinosaur social life over the years, with dinosaur nests and young found in Montana, USA, and in Patagonia, Argentina. Fossils of herds have shown that duckbills of North America moved about in herds and family groups. We have also found out that some of the more active meat-eaters hunted in packs, like wolves.

Sharing the landscape

The first finds in North America showed how all kinds of dinosaurs lived together in one place. Big, plant-eating sauropods, such as *Apatasaurus* and *Argentinosaurus*, browsed the higher vegetation. Smaller ornithopods, including

Allosaurus skeleton

the duckbills, ate the lower-growing plants. Large meat-eaters, such as *Allosaurus, Giganotosaurus* and *Tyrannosaurus*, lived by hunting down other animals. The deposits from the end of the age of dinosaurs show the spectacular development of horned and armoured dinosaurs. Horns and armour against teeth and claws – it was an arms race!

Different then from now

The modern-day sites that show the best dinosaur fossils are totally different from what they were like in dinosaur times. The Hell Creek area of the USA and the Patagonia region of Argentina are now arid badlands, with no large animals living there at all. In the Cretaceous period, these regions had woodlands and rivers, and were populated by herds of huge dinosaurs.

Heart of the dinosaurs

Despite the find of a possible *Thescelosaurus* heart at Hell Creek, there is still a debate as to whether dinosaurs were cold-blooded, warm-blooded or something in-between. Future fossil finds may help to clear up this mystery.

Go further...

Hunt dinosaurs in the desert: www.desertusa.com/mag98/dec/stories/dinosafari.html

Read about the 19th-century 'bone wars': www.levins.com/bwars.shtml

Read an interview with Luis Chiappé about discovering the titanosaur nursery: www.amnh.org/exhibitions/expeditions/dinosaur/patagonia/environment.html

Uncover T Rex by Dennis Schatz and Davide Bonadonna (Bookwise International, 2003)

Where to Find Dinosaurs Today by Daniel Cohen and Susan Cohen (Puffin, 1992)

Dinosaur hunter
Looks for dinosaur bones. Some hunters study the bones that they find themselves; others sell them or bring them back to be prepared in the laboratory and then studied in detail by palaeontologists.

Excavator
Digs things out of the ground.

Ichnologist
Studies footprints and trackways. Such work is especially valuable for studying the lifestyles of dinosaurs.

Professor
Heads a department in a university or college, or is a teacher there at the highest level.

See the best collection of North American dinosaurs at: Tyrrell Museum of Palaeontology, Drumheller, Alberta T0J 0Y0, Canada Telephone +1 403 823 8899 www.tyrrellmuseum.com

View *Tyrannosaurus* skeletons on display in the: Black Hills Institute of Geological Research, Hill City, South Dakota, USA Telephone +1 605 574 4289 www.bhigr.com

Find out more about the Dinosaur National Monument at: The Dinosaur Quarry Visitor Center, Jensen, Utah 84035, USA Telephone +1 435 781 7700 www.nps.gov/dino/

Minmi, an armoured dinosaur that lived
in Australia in the Early Cretaceous

CHAPTER 4

Africa &
Australia

Africa and Australia were part of the
southern landmass of Gondwana in
dinosaur times. While Gondwana was part
of the bigger supercontinent of Pangaea,
the dinosaurs that lived there were similar
to those in other parts of the world.
However, as time went on, and Gondwana
separated from Laurasia, these southern
dinosaurs developed different species from
those in the north. For a long time,
dinosaurs had been found on every
continent of the world except Antarctica.
However, since the 1970s dinosaur fossils
have been found on the great Antarctic
continent. Of course, at the time of the
dinosaurs, Antarctica was not the frozen
icecap that it is now. However, the
dinosaur fossils found in southern
Australia show that some dinosaurs
were adapted to very cold conditions.

Dinosaur teeth

Carnivorous dinosaurs evolved efficient meat slicers long before the invention of steak knives. A serrated edge is best for slicing through flesh. The largest predatory dinosaurs, such as North Africa's Carchardontosaurus, housed their teeth in massive jaws. Carchardontosaurus had a mouth that was large enough to hold a seven-year-old child, and some of its teeth were the length of a human hand. This four-tonne predator's slashing bite would have been devastating.

Teeth for plants

Plant-eating dinosaurs had different kinds of teeth. Prosauropods' teeth were coarsely serrated, like vegetable shredders. Sauropods raked leaves from trees with comb-like teeth. Ornithischians had beaks for gathering food, and teeth that could either grind or chop. Ornithischians also had cheeks to hold the food while chewing.

▼ This *Carchardontosaurus* skull is shown beside a human skull for scale. *Carchardontosaurus* was a terrifying meat-eater that ran down its prey, pounding along on massive, muscular hind legs.

▼ Paul Sereno shows off the fossilized *Sarcosuchus* skeleton that he discovered in the Sahara. SuperCroc was the length of a bus and probably weighed 8 tonnes.

SuperCroc

Fifty years before Paul Sereno found a whole *Sarcosuchus* skeleton, French palaeontologist Albert-Félix de Lapparent (1905–1975) found fossil crocodile teeth in the Sahara. How did he know they came from a giant crocodile and not a meat-eating dinosaur? Easy! Crocodile teeth are straight, while most dinosaur teeth are curved – but both kinds are just as good for killing and ripping up big prey. In Cretaceous times the Sahara was not a desert. It was a tropical plain, criss-crossed by tree-lined rivers and streams. It was also home to plenty of dinosaurs on which *Sarcosuchus* could feast.

▶ Like this modern crocodile, *Sarcosuchus* had upward-pointing eye sockets, so it probably relied on the same hunting technique. It would have waited just beneath the surface, ready to ambush dinosaurs and other prey that came to the riverbank to drink.

Fast-moving plant-eaters

During the Jurassic, southern Africa was brutally hot. Most of the dinosaurs that lived there were small, dog-sized plant-eaters. *Lesothosaurus* and its close relative, *Fabrosaurus*, were bird-hipped dinosaurs that could run fast on their hind legs, using their long tails for balance. *Heterodontosaurus* was another small, agile plant-eater.

Scrubland plants

Early Jurassic southern Africa was a semi desert with a sparse, scrubby covering of cycads, conifers and ferns. The supercontinent of Pangaea still existed and inland climates could be harsh and hot. Certain dinosaurs may have aestivated – slept during the hottest times of the year. Some scientists suggest that the teeth of *Heterodontosaurus* could not have grown properly unless there were long aestivation periods when they were not being used.

▲ In the open landscapes of the Early Jurassic, danger could be seen coming from a long way away. Early plant-eaters such as *Lesothosaurus* evolved long legs to run to safety.

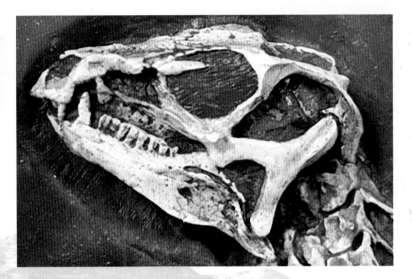

Lumbering plant-eaters

Not all of the Early Jurassic plant-eaters were small and speedy. Prosauropods, relatives of the huge sauropods, appeared in Africa around this time. *Massospondylus* was a cow-sized prosauropod, able to walk on all fours or up on its hind legs. It had teeth adapted for shredding plant matter, and it also swallowed stones that helped to pulp tough vegetable fibres in its gizzard (pre-stomach).

◄ This skull belongs to *Heterodontosaurus*, or 'different tooth lizard'. The dinosaur had small teeth at the front of its mouth for snipping off leaves and stems, and tall square ones at the back for grinding up plant fibres. It also had two pairs of longer teeth, or tusks, perhaps for fighting rivals.

▲ As well as being equipped with three kinds of teeth, *Heterodontosaurus* may have also had cheek pouches. It could have used the pouches to push plant matter over its back teeth.

Neck rib

Windpipe protected by
muscle and neck ribs

▼ *Rapetosaurus* did not chew its food. Instead, like all
sauropods, it swallowed stones to grind up the plant food in
its stomach. Modern plant-eating birds also do this. We find
out about dinosaur food and digestion by looking at fossil
teeth and coprolite (fossil dung).

Horsey nostrils

Peg-like teeth

Muscles from
shoulder blade
power front leg

Gizzard

Madagascan giant

Titanosaurs were sauropods that
flourished over most of the world for
200 million years. They had long necks
and tails, and they browsed on leafy
vegetation. Palaeontologists have identified
more than 30 kinds of titanosaur, but
almost all are known from only a few
bones. The most complete titanosaur
specimen was a skeleton of *Rapetosaurus*,
found on the island of Madagascar.

Massive lungs for
extracting oxygen
from air

Heart for pumping
oxygen-rich blood
around the body

Brain power

Relative to its body size, a titanosaur's brain was small.
Finding food did not demand much brain power because
plants were plentiful. *Rapetosaurus* needed some intelligence
to evade predators, but mostly it relied on size. Growth
patterns in the bones show that, by the time it was 12 years
old, it was too big for most meat-eaters. *Tyrannosaurus* and
other hunters needed much bigger brains relative to their
size so that they could outwit their food – other dinosaurs!

Bulky burden

Sauropods were the biggest land animals ever. Experts
originally thought that they must have inhabited swamps
and lakes, where water could support their bulk. Now we
know they did walk on land, because of fossil trackways
and bones found in dry habitats. Some palaeontologists
argue that sauropods had air sacs, like modern birds. Air
sacs make birds' lungs more efficient and also save weight,
replacing some of the bone mass with air. If sauropods
had air sacs, their bodies would have been much lighter
than they appeared.

MEET THE EXPERT: KRISTI CURRY ROGERS

Palaeontologist Kristi Curry Rogers, shown here with a theropod, has been fascinated by dinosaurs since she was six years old. She discovered and named the titanosaur *Rapetosaurus* and is still doing research on Madagascan dinosaurs. Her special interest is histology (tissue structures). She studies bone structures and, from this, is able to interpret how long-extinct animals, particularly the sauropods, grew and lived.

Large stomach for processing vegetation

Backbone has broad projections where muscles attach

◀ Like muscles, internal organs usually rotted away rather than becoming fossils. However, we can guess from its size that *Rapetosaurus* would have needed a huge heart to pump blood round that great body. Its lungs must have been enormous, too.

Titanosaur's tail shorter than in other sauropods

Lizard-like hip bone

Huge thigh bone to support 20-tonne body weight

Foot supported by a thick pad of gristle

◀ *Rapetosaurus* was named after Rapeto, a mischievous giant from Madagascan folk stories. The *Rapetosaurus* skeleton that Kristi Curry Rogers found in 2001 measured 6m from head to tail and belonged to an individual that was just a few years old. Adults grew to 15m long.

◀ Muscles rarely fossilize, but we can see where bands of tissue called tendons attached them to the bones. From these muscle 'scars', we can work out how the muscles were laid out and how the animal moved.

Dinosaur tracks

Australia has some of the best fossilized dinosaur tracks in the world, including very rare stegosaur prints. The trackways at Broome, Western Australia, and Lark Quarry, Queensland, have thousands of dinosaur prints. Ichnology – the study of fossil tracks – reveals a lot about dinosaur behaviour.

Studying tracks

When footprints of many individuals of the same kind of dinosaur are often found together, it shows that they lived in herds. Long trackways can indicate that dinosaurs migrated for hundreds or thousands of kilometres. The trackway at Broome covers an 80km stretch of coastline. We cannot tell exactly what animals made the prints, but we can see what types of dinosaurs were involved. The biggest prints, which were 80cm long, were made by massive sauropods. There were also 53cm-long prints from big theropods, prints from small, active ornithopods and a set that may have come from a stegosaur.

small ornithopod

small theropod

Lark Quarry

In the 1960s, thousands of fossil footprints were found in Lark Quarry, Queensland, by a local farm manager. The quarry was named after Malcolm Lark, a volunteer who helped to excavate the site. The footprints tell of herds of small ornithopods (similar to *Hypsilophodon*) and small unidentified theropods drinking from a Cretaceous stream. Suddenly, they were spooked by the appearance of a big predator (a tyrannosaur), and they ran about in confusion, scattering in a frenzied stampede.

◀ The footprints in the sandstone of Lark Quarry look like a jumbled mess. However, with careful study, scientists have managed to piece together a dramatic story depicting herds of dinosaurs fleeing in panic from a hunter.

tyrannosaur

FOOTPRINT SHAPES

Ornithopods walked on two legs. Their footprints have three toes, rather like those of theropods, but with blunter claws.

Theropods stood on their hind legs and could run fast. Their print showed three long toes, like birds, their descendants.

Sauropods walked on all fours with their tails up, not sweeping the ground. The biggest prints are more than 1.5m wide.

Polar dinosaurs

In dinosaur times, the poles were warmer than they are today, although they were still cold. Polar dinosaurs had to cope with months of darkness, lit only by the Moon and eerie southern lights. Dinosaur Cove, near Melbourne, is a time capsule of fossils that formed when Australia was farther south and within the Antarctic Circle. Since the 1970s, palaeontologists have also discovered dinosaur fossils in Antarctica.

▲ A dinosaur warning sign stands by the road that leads to Dinosaur Cove. The dinosaurs that lived there 100 million years ago were very different from the *Stegosaurus* shown on the sign. They had evolved special ways of surviving the cold and long, dark winters.

**MEET THE EXPERT:
PATRICIA VICKERS-RICH**

The excavations at Dinosaur Cove were led by geologist and palaeontologist Patricia Vickers-Rich and her husband, Tom Rich, curator of the Museum of Victoria. They named one of their major discoveries *Leaellynasaura* after their daughter Leaellyn, and another *Timimus* after their son Tim.

Dinosaur Cove

The Dinosaur Cove fossils were in very hard layers of rock, halfway up a cliff. The palaeontologists blasted their way into the cliff-face using explosives and heavy mining equipment. These Cretaceous rocks formed on the floor of a rift valley as Australia tore itself away from the continent of Antarctica, far to the south of where it now lies.

▲ In 2004, palaeontologist William Hammer revisited the site on Antarctica's mainland where, 13 years earlier, he had discovered *Cryolophosaurus*, a crested meat-eating dinosaur from the Early Jurassic. On this second expedition he found the remains of another, as yet unnamed, theropod.

◀ To gather every scrap of light *Leaellynasaura* had huge eyes, and the parts of its brain devoted to vision were enlarged. It had a long tail and a small head and arms – rather like a kangaroo! It shared the gloom with the strange, armoured *Atlascopcosaurus*, ostrich-like *Timimus* and a small, unnamed allosaur.

Antarctic finds

During the Mesozoic, Antarctica was farther north than it is today, and it had warm, moist climates. There is not much of Antarctica that is not covered by ice, so it is difficult to get at the rocks and fossils beneath. However, since the 1980s the bare, ice-free rocks of Vega Island, off the eastern side of the Antarctic peninsula, have yielded duck-billed dinosaurs and sea reptiles, while James Ross Island has produced a theropod and a nodosaurid ankylosaur. Perhaps the most spectacular find was that of the crested meat-eater *Cryolophosaurus*, on the mainland in 1991.

SUMMARY OF CHAPTER 4: AFRICA & AUSTRALIA

The path of evolution

At the beginning of the age of the dinosaurs, the time of Pangaea, the dinosaurs on the modern continents of Africa, Australia and Antarctica were not much different from those in other lands. The small, fast movers of southern Africa were similar to those of Europe and North America. In the Late Jurassic, the dinosaurs of East Africa included huge sauropods such as *Brachiosaurus*, spiky stegosaurs such as *Kentrosaurus* and fierce meat-eaters such as *Allosaurus* – a similar mix to those of North America at the same time. Later, as the continents split up, dinosaurs began to evolve along their own separate lines. By the Cretaceous, big plant-eaters called titanosaurs lived on Madagascar (now an island off the southeastern coast of Africa). Like South America, where titanosaurs have also been found, Africa and Madagascar were part of the supercontinent of Gondwana at the time.

An amazing mix

Not all the big meat-eaters were dinosaurs. *Sarcosuchus*, the biggest crocodile the world has ever known, lived in Africa and probably fed on dinosaurs. Although we think of dinosaurs and other reptiles as being adapted to hot environments, we have found that the southern tip of Australia had a chill Antarctic climate in Cretaceous times. But we have also discovered that this area had its own dinosaur population. Dinosaurs were more adaptable than we have given them credit for.

The backbone of an Early Cretaceous plant-eater, *Ouranosaurus*, sticks out of the desert sand in Niger, Africa. Since the 1990s, there have been many exciting dinosaur discoveries in the Sahara Desert.

Go further...

An account of Australian dinosaurs: home.alphalink. com.au/~dannj/

See Antarctic dinosaurs at: antarcticsun.usap.gov/oldissues2002-2003/Sun111002/dinosaurs.html

Dinosaur Atlas by John Malam and John Woodward (Dorling Kindersley, 2006)

Dinosaur Worlds: Rise of the Dinosaurs by Don Lessem (Heinemann, 1996)

Histologist
Studies tissues, especially bone tissues, to discover information about growth rates. Histology reveals how long dinosaurs lived, and even in what kind of conditions (bones may stop growing for a time if food is scarce or the climate is cold).

Palaeobiologist
Studies the origins of life, and the growth and structure of fossil animals as living organisms.

Volunteer
Works for no money – just for the interest of the job. Volunteers often work at dig sites.

Mounted skeletons from East Africa can be seen in: Humboldt Museum of Natural History, Invaliden-strasse 43, D-10115 Berlin, Germany Telephone: +49 (0)30 2093 8591 www.naturkundemuseum-berlin.de

See early African dinosaurs at: South African Museum, 25 Queen Victoria Street, Cape Town, South Africa Telephone: +27 (0)21 481 3800 www.iziko.org.za/sam

The best place for Australian dinosaurs is: National Dinosaur Museum, Gold Creek Road and Barton Highway, Canberra, Australia Telephone: +61 (0)2 6230 2655 www.nationaldinosaurmuseum. com.au

TIMELINE

MESOZOIC ERA	**CRETACEOUS PERIOD**	**65 MYA**	End of the Age of Reptiles. Dinosaurs, pterosaurs, swimming reptiles and many other groups suddenly die out. Other kinds of animal are also badly hit: birds and marsupial mammals each lose 75 per cent of their species, while placental mammals lose 14 per cent. Despite these losses, birds and mammals eventually recover to repopulate the world.	***Tyrannosaurus rex***
		80 MYA	The continents are well scattered, with more individual landmasses than today. Different kinds of dinosaurs appear on different landmasses, evolving in isolation from one another. South America is an island continent. Eastern and western North America are separated by shallow sea, but western North America is still attached to Asia.	***Protoceratops***
		100 MYA	Flowering plants become widespread. The main type of landscape is forests of broadleaved trees with an undergrowth of floral herbs. Dinosaurs evolve into ground-feeding and low-browsing types, such as duckbills, ceratopsians and armoured dinosaurs. Coniferous trees – and the high-browsing dinosaurs that feed on them – become restricted to upland areas.	***Tenontosaurus***
		120 MYA	The climate is warm and moist. Gondwana breaks up as South America separates from Africa, and India separates from Australia and Antarctica. Sea level is generally low, but it begins to rise as the period progresses. Different kinds of birds evolve, particularly in China, which is also home to feathered dinosaurs such as *Microraptor*.	***Microraptor***
	JURASSIC PERIOD	**145 MYA**	The end of the Jurassic period and the beginning of the Cretaceous. This is the heyday of the long-necked plant-eating sauropods such as *Brachiosaurus*, and of the tall coniferous trees that they feed upon. An extinction in the oceans marks the end of the Jurassic, with some 30 per cent of species dying out. Birds evolve from theropod dinosaurs.	***Brachiosaurus***
		160 MYA	The South Atlantic Ocean begins to open up, creating rift valleys in Gondwana. North America remains connected to Europe by a land bridge. Sea level is quite high, with many shallow coastal seas and a wide variety of marine animals. The Rocky Mountains begin to rise. Climates are generally moist. Theropods such as *Megalosaurus* are the main predators.	***Megalosaurus***
		175 MYA	Sudden flourishing of the long-necked sauropods and the large meat-eaters that prey upon them. Insects such as dragonflies and cockroaches are plentiful. The Tethys Ocean separates Pangaea into Laurasia and Gondwana. This ocean is home to various marine reptiles, such as ichthyosaurs, which had first appeared 250 million years ago.	***Ichthyosaurus***
		180 MYA	New ammonite species appear, following the end-Triassic extinction. Dinosaurs flourish and take the places of other reptile groups. Amongst the dinosaurs, plated stegosaurs appear as well as the two-legged heterodontosaurs. Inland climates remain dry, especially in North America and southern Africa.	***Scelidosaurus***
	TRIASSIC PERIOD	**208 MYA**	End of the Triassic period and beginning of the Jurassic. Mass extinction affects 65 per cent of marine species and a large number of land species. The first true mammals appear and survive the extinction. Pangaea is still in one piece but the Tethys Ocean partly separates it into a northern part, Laurasia, and a southern part, Gondwana.	***Morganucodon***
		210 MYA	Flying archosaurs called pterosaurs appear. Conifers become the main plant form as seed ferns die out. Reptiles that feed on the seed ferns also die back, allowing the dinosaurs to flourish. Rift valleys begin to appear across Pangaea. Crocodile-like reptiles include groups that will become extinct at the end of the Triassic, such as rauisuchians like 5m-long *Prestosuchus*.	***Prestosuchus***
		230 MYA	Seed ferns take over from the club mosses as the main plants. The centre of Pangaea is so far from the sea that it is arid and lifeless. Life flourishes around the edges of the continent, where the climate is seasonal. Archosaurs begin to split into the crocodile group and the dinosaur group, which includes *Eoraptor* (one of the earliest-known dinosaurs).	***Eoraptor***
		250 MYA	Beginning of the Triassic period. All the landmasses are joined in the supercontinent of Pangaea. Animal life is recovering after a mass extinction at the end of the Permian, which wiped out up to 95 per cent of species. Archosaurs are the main surviving group of reptiles. As in the preceding periods, the most widespread plants are the club mosses.	**Club moss**

Glossary

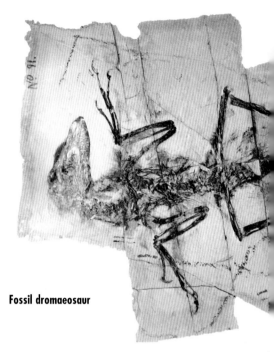

Fossil dromaeosaur

aestivate
To sleep away the hot summer months.

ammonite
An extinct shellfish in a coiled shell that was common in the Mesozoic.

ankylosaur
An armoured ornithischian dinosaur that had bony plates on its back.

badlands
Areas of wasteland and worn-away rock, which are literally 'bad land' to cross.

belemnite
An extinct shellfish with a bullet-shaped shell that was common in the Mesozoic.

camouflage
Colour or pattern that makes something difficult to see against its background.

carnivore
A flesh-eating animal.

ceratopsian
An ornithischian dinosaur that had a head shield and sometimes horns.

climate
The average weather conditions of an area over a long period of time.

cold-blooded
Describes an animal that cannot control its body temperature. Fish, amphibians and modern reptiles are cold-blooded.

comet
A space body of ice and rock.

conifer
An evergreen tree that reproduces by cones, for example pine and cypress.

coprolite
Fossilized dung.

Cretaceous
The time from 145 to 65 million years ago, and the third of the three periods that make up the Mesozoic era.

cycad
A primitive plant, related to conifers but resembling a palm tree.

dromaeosaur
A small theropod dinosaur with an outsize claw on each hind foot.

duckbill
An ornithopod dinosaur that had a duck-like beak and, usually, a head crest.

environment
The total conditions of a place – its landscape, climate, plants and animal life.

evolve
To change from one species to another over millions of years, by passing on useful characteristics from one generation to the next.

extinct
Describes an animal or plant that has died out globally, never to reappear.

fossil
The remains of an animal or plant that died long ago, preserved in rock.

gizzard
In some dinosaurs and birds, a muscular pouch that holds swallowed stones to grind food before it enters the stomach.

Gondwana
The southern landmass created by the break-up of Pangaea.

ichthyosaur
A dolphin-like, predatory marine reptile that lived in the Mesozoic.

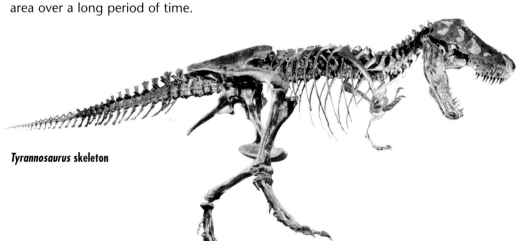

Tyrannosaurus **skeleton**

Jurassic
The time from 206 to 145 million years ago, and the second of the three periods that make up the Mesozoic era.

KT boundary
The rock layer that marks the time when dinosaurs became extinct, the end of the Cretaceous and beginning of the Tertiary.

Laurasia
The northern landmass created by the break-up of Pangaea.

Mesozoic era
The period of geological time stretching from 251 to 65 million years ago.

metabolism
The physical and chemical systems that keep an animal or plant alive.

mosasaur
A giant, predatory marine lizard that lived in the Cretaceous.

nothosaur
A fish-eating marine reptile that lived in Triassic seas.

ornithischian
Describes the group of dinosaurs that had hip bones arranged like those of a bird. The ornithischians were made up of the ornithopods, pachycephalosaurs, ceratopsians, stegosaurs and ankylosaurs. They were all plant-eaters.

ornithopod
A two-legged ornithischian dinosaur.

palaeontologist
A scientist who studies fossils.

Pangaea
The supercontinent that was around from about 270 to 175 million years ago, made up of all the world's landmasses.

placodont
A turtle-like reptile from the Triassic.

plesiosaur
A long-necked, predatory marine reptile that lived in the Jurassic and Cretaceous.

pliosaur
A short-necked marine reptile, related to plesiosaurs, that lived in the Mesozoic.

prosauropod
A large, long-necked, plant-eating saurischian dinosaur that walked on two legs or on all fours.

pterosaur
A flying reptile with wings made from skin stretched over a long fourth finger.

saurischian
Describes the group of dinosaurs that had hip bones arranged like those of a lizard. The saurischians were made up of the theropods (which gave rise to birds) and sauropods.

sauropod
A huge, long-necked, plant-eating saurischian dinosaur, that walked on all fours, related to the prosauropods.

stegosaur
An ornithischian dinosaur that had plates on its back.

supercontinent
A landmass containing more than one continental plate.

Tertiary
The period of geological time after the Mesozoic, from 65 to 2 million years ago.

theropod
A two-legged, carnivorous saurischian dinosaur with sharp teeth and claws.

Triassic
The time from 251 to 206 million years ago, and the first of the three periods that make up the Mesozoic era, when early dinosaurs appeared.

tyrannosaur
A large, flesh-eating theropod dinosaur.

Eoraptor skull

vertebrate
An animal with a backbone.

volcano
A hole (vent) through which gas, ash and molten rock erupt on to Earth's surface and may build up to form a mountain.

warm-blooded
Describes an animal that can keep its body temperature the same, whatever the surrounding temperature. Birds and mammals are warm-blooded.

Index

Acknowledgements

The publisher would like to thank the following for permission to reproduce their material. Every care has been taken to trace copyright holders. However, if there have been unintentional omissions or failure to trace copyright holders, we apologize and will, if informed, endeavour to make corrections in any future edition.

Key: *b* = bottom, *c* = centre, *l* = left, *r* = right, *t* = top

1 Natural History Museum, London; 2–3 Corbis/Louie Psihoyos; 7 Dean Steadman/Kingfisher; 13*tl* Corbis/Walter Geiersperger; 13*tr* Dean Steadman/Kingfisher; 13*cr* Photolibrary/Jeremy Woodhouse; 14 Getty/National Geographic Society; 15 Loïc Bazalgette, Laboratoire Dynamique de la lithosphère, Université Montpellier II; 16 Natural History Museum, London; 16–17 Corbis/Ladislav Janicek/zefa; 18*bl* Mike Hettwer; 18–19 Getty/Louie Psihoyos; 20*tl* Getty/AFP; 20*b* Natural History Museum, London; 21*t* American Museum of Natural History, Washington; 22*t* Corbis/Xinhua; 22*b* Getty/Xu Xing; 24*bl* Photolibrary/Satoshi Kuribayashi; 25 Science Photo Library/Jim Amos; 27 Natural History Museum, London; 28 Natural History Museum, London; 29 Getty/Richard Nowitz; 30 DK Images; 31 Dean Steadman/Kingfisher; 33*tr* Science Photo Library/Smithsonian Institution; 34 Don Lessum, Dino Don Inc.; 34*tr* Empics/AP/Mariano Izquierdo; 35 Science Photo Library/Carlos Goldin; 36 Dean Steadman/Kingfisher; 36–37 Dean Steadman/Kingfisher; 37 Empics/AP/Karen Tam; 37*b* Corbis/Louie Psihoyos; 40–41 Impossible Pictures; 40*bl* Natural History Museum, London; 41*t* Natural History Museum, London; 42*bl* Corbis/Louie Psihoyos; 44 Science Photo Library/Christian Darkin; 45 Jim Page/North Carolina Museum of Natural Sciences; 46 Getty/Louie Psihoyos; 47 Queensland Museum, Australia; 48*bl* Getty/Louie Psihoyos; 48–49 Empics/AP/Rick Bowmer; 49*t* Corbis/Sygma; 49*b* Science Photo Library/Tom McHugh; 51*t* University of California Museum of Palaeontology; 53 Empics/AP/Gail Burton; 54–55 Wildlight/Philip Quirk; 55*t* Corbis/John Noble; 56*bl* AAP Image/Julian Smith; 56 Corbis/Frans Lanting; 56*tr* Science Photo Library/Peter Menzel; 57*t* Empics/AP/Augustane College; 58*b* Getty/Stephen Wilkes; 58–59*t* Getty/AFP; 59*br* Corbis/Louie Psihoyos; 62–63 Loïc Bazalgette, Laboratoire Dynamique de la lithosphère, Université Montpellier II; 64 Getty/Louie Psihoyos.

The publisher would like to thank the following illustrators: Rebecca Painter 9*br*, 36*cl*, 55*b*; Sebastien Quigley (Linden Artists) 18–19; Sam Weston (Linden Artists) 8–9, 12–13, 16–17, 24–25, 26–27, 38–39, 42–43, 50–51; Sam Weston and Steve Weston (Linden Artists) 20–21, 34–35; Steve Weston (Linden Artists) Cover, 4–5, 11, 22–23, 30–31, 32–33, 44–45*c*, 52–53, 54–55, 56–57; Peter Winfield 10, 15, 17*r*, 19*r*, 26*b*, 29, 45*r*, 47, 59.

The publisher would also like to thank Kristi Curry Rogers for her assistance with pages 52–53 and David Varrichio for his assistance with page 18.